WONDERFUL WORMS

WONDERFUL WORMS

BY LINDA GLASER
PICTURES BY LORETTA KRUPINSKI

THE MILLBROOK PRESS • BROOKFIELD, CONNECTICUT

TO MY PARENTS,
WHOSE LOVE OF NATURE HAS
OPENED WORLDS TO ME

Library of Congress Cataloging-in-Publication Data
Glaser, Linda.
Wonderful worms / by Linda Glaser ; illustrated
by Loretta Krupinski.
        p.   cm.
Summary: Describes the physical characteristics,
behavior, and life cycle of the common earthworm.
ISBN 1-56294-062-7 (LIB.)   ISBN 1-56294-703-6 (TR.)
ISBN 1-56294-730-3 (PBK. ED.)
1. Earthworms—Juvenile literature.   [1. Earthworms.]
I. Krupinski, Loretta, ill. II. Title.

QL391.A6G53   1992
595.1—dc20   91-38752   CIP   AC

The Millbrook Press
2 Old New Milford Road
Brookfield, Connecticut 06804
Printed in the United States of America
6

Earthworms are fat and wiggly
like my fingers and toes.

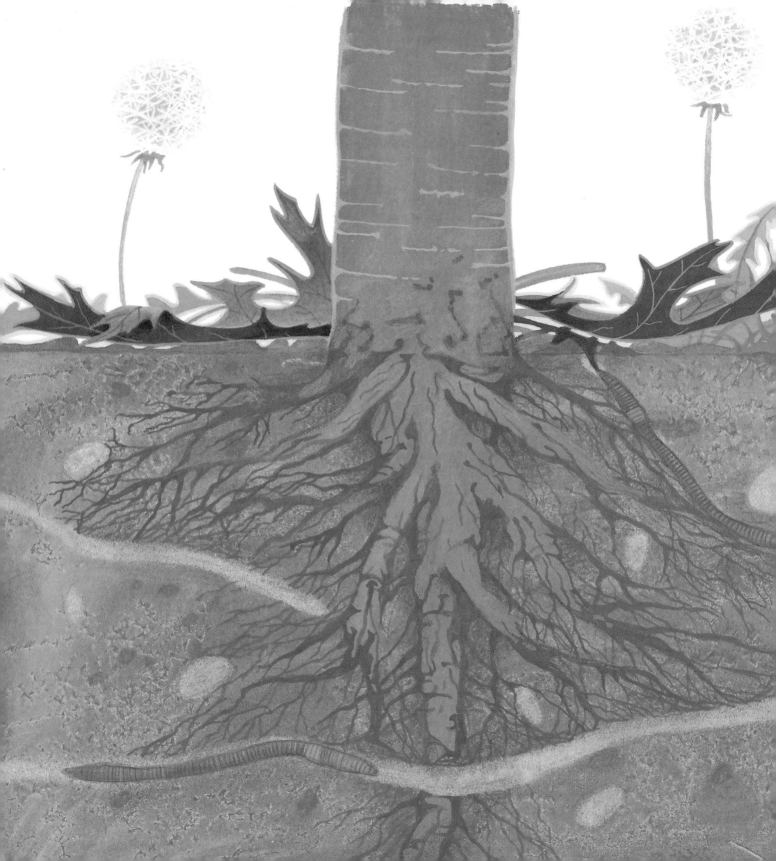

**They live where it is cool and dark and damp,
where roots spread out like underground trees.**

Worms feel sounds with their whole bodies.
They feel thunder when I walk.

They are wonderful diggers.
They dig passageways and burrows.

**But they don't use shovels
or fingers or toes.**

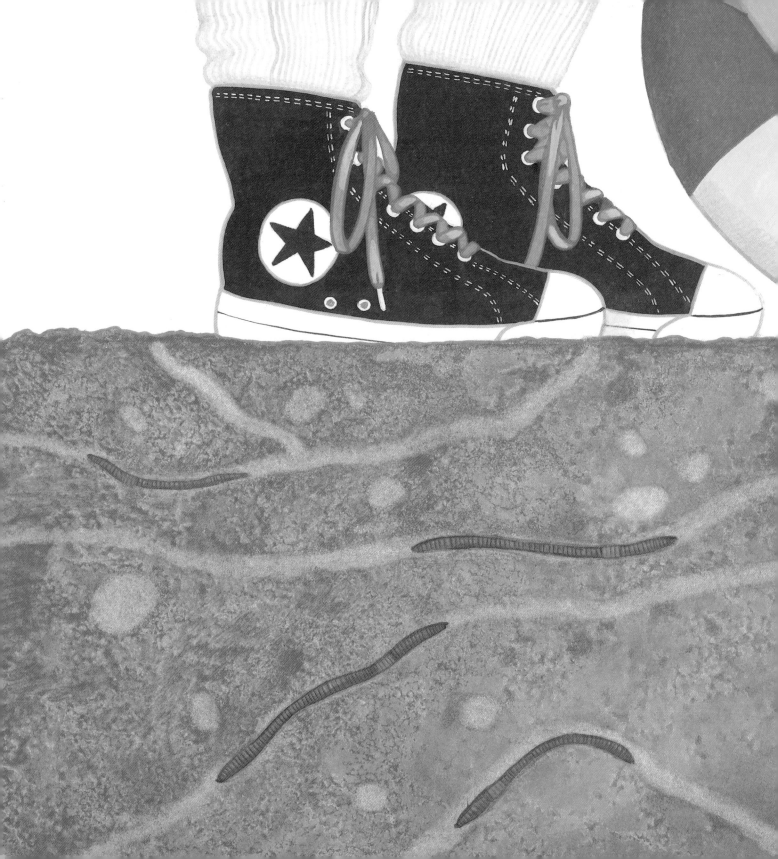

How do they do it?
They eat their way through and move along.

They stretch out, long and thin,
and squeeze in, short and fat.

Stretch and squeeze, stretch and squeeze.
Eat and dig, move and dig.

**Earthworms mix and turn the dirt
as they dig and tunnel in the earth.**

They make the soil soft and airy
so the roots of plants can breathe and grow.

Worms don't have eyes or ears or a nose.
They do have a mouth.

And they need food, just like I do.
But they eat dirt and rotting leaves.

They swallow tiny pieces.
And inside the worms, the food changes.

**When it comes out of their tail ends,
it makes the earth rich so plants can grow.**

Earthworms are my helpers, the underground gardeners.
We work hard in the dirt in my garden, their home.

FACTS ABOUT WONDERFUL WORMS

For young children who want to know more about earthworms, here are some simple answers to common questions they may have.

Do earthworms bite people?

No. Earthworms don't bite anyone because they don't have teeth.

Why are earthworms so slimy?

Their skin needs to be moist in order to breathe. That's because earthworms breathe through their skin. Also, moist skin makes it easier for earthworms to move through their burrows. If an earthworm dries out, it will die.

Why does a worm's skin sometimes feel rough?

If you gently move your finger along a worm's "belly side" from the tail end forward, it does feel rough. That's because worms have many bristles called *setae*. These bristles help the worm cling to its burrow when a bird or other creature is trying to pull it out. The bristles also help the worm move inside the burrow.

If an earthworm breaks in two, does it really become two worms?

No. But if it breaks off close to the head or close to the tail, it won't die. Instead, it will grow another head or tail! However, the shorter broken piece won't grow into another whole worm.

How long do earthworms live?

They have been known to live more than ten years. But most earthworms live less than a year.

Which animals eat worms?

Birds, lizards, centipedes, frogs, toads, turtles, skunks, snakes, gophers, and moles all eat worms. In fact, moles catch earthworms and store them in their own burrows so that they'll have them to eat when they get hungry.

Which animal is the most dangerous to earthworms?

People who spray insecticides (bug-killer poisons) on the earth are the biggest danger to earthworms. That's because poisons can kill many acres of worms at one time. And there can be over a million earthworms in one acre of fertile land!

Where do earthworms go in winter?

They go down below the frost line and curl up in their burrows.

What is that fat lump on the worm's body?

It is called a *clitellum*. All adult earthworms have one. The clitellum produces a ring-like band after a worm mates. The ring moves forward, collecting eggs, and slips over the worm's head. As it slides off, the ends seal and form a cocoon. Baby worms hatch from this cocoon.

Where do baby worms come from?

They come from eggs. The eggs are inside a small, round cocoon. There are between one and twenty eggs in one cocoon. But often only one or two eggs hatch. When they hatch, the baby earthworms are thin and white.

What type of worm is in a ''wormy'' apple?

It is not really a worm. It is a type of caterpillar. There are many insects that are called worms that aren't true worms, such as apple worms, inchworms, tomato worms, and mealworms. You can tell that they aren't really worms because they all have little legs. And they eventually turn into something else—such as butterflies, moths, or beetles. Worms don't have any legs and they never turn into anything else. They stay worms their whole lives.

Are there other types of worms?

Yes. There are many types including round-worms, ribbonworms, flatworms, fanworms, and segmented worms. The earthworm is a type of segmented worm. There are about 12,000 types of segmented worms. A common one is the brandling, which is used for composting. An unusual one that lives in Australia is the giant Australian earthworm. It can grow to be over nine feet long!

Why do worms come out when it rains?

It's believed that they come out because their burrows are flooded and the water is no longer fresh.

Why don't we see more worms outside during the day?

Worms are night animals. Because there is a danger of drying out during the day, they poke out of their burrows to find something to eat at night.

How can you tell which end is the worm's head?

The head is slightly pointed. And that lump called the clitellum is closer to the head end of adult earthworms.

Do worms have a top side and a bottom side?

Yes. The bottom side is often a little paler than the top side. If you put a worm on its top side it will quickly turn onto its ''belly side''.

Does it hurt a worm to be put on a fishing hook?

Worms have sensory organs that make their skin very sensitive to the touch. And they do wriggle when they are put on a fishing hook. But we don't actually know what worms feel.

How can one little worm really help in a big garden?

One earthworm can't do much by itself. But in one yard there can be thousands of earthworms. Together they mix the soil, supply it with air, and fertilize it. All this helps plants to grow. So earthworms are very important. Without them, our earth might not be the rich and beautiful source of life that it is.

ABOUT THE AUTHOR AND ARTIST

LINDA GLASER has had an organic garden and a worm compost pile for over ten years. During that time she has come to value the amazing work that worms do for our earth.

Ms. Glaser teaches English, Children's Literature, and Creative Writing at Vista Community College in Berkeley, California. She is the author of another children's book, *Keep Your Socks on, Albert.*

Ms. Glaser lives in Berkeley with her husband, John, and their two young daughters.

LORETTA KRUPINSKI is also an avid gardener and claims to have encountered many worms in the process.

A resident of Old Lyme, Connecticut, she is a professional maritime artist, a vocation that grew out of her love of sailing. That interest is expressed in two of her recent picture books, *Lost in the Fog*, which she adapted and illustrated, and *Sailing to the Sea*, which she illustrated.